Digital Guardians:

A Guide to Cyber Hygiene for Parents

Author:

L. Randolf Bryant

Digital Guardians: A Guide to Cyber Hygiene for Parents

Table of Contents

Introduction:

In this age of rapid technological advancement, the digital world has become an integral part of our daily lives. From the way we communicate and learn to how we work and play, technology has transformed every facet of our existence. While these changes bring incredible opportunities, they also usher in new challenges, especially for parents tasked with safeguarding their children in this brave new digital frontier.

Welcome to "Digital Guardians: A Guide to Cyber Hygiene for Parents." In the pages that follow, we will embark on a journey to navigate the digital age together. Just as parents have protected and guided their children through the physical world, it's now essential to extend that care into the digital realm.

Our goal is to equip you with the knowledge, skills, and resources necessary to be vigilant digital guardians for your family. We'll explore the ins and outs of cyber hygiene, a set of practices and principles that will empower you to foster a safe and responsible digital environment for your loved ones.

But before we delve into the intricacies of cyber hygiene, let's take a moment to reflect on the profound impact of the Digital Age on our lives and why it's crucial to adapt, embrace, and, above all, protect in this ever-evolving landscape.

So, let's embark on this digital journey together, where the possibilities are endless, the challenges are real, and the role of a digital guardian becomes more critical than ever before. Welcome to the future— welcome to the pages of "Digital Guardians."

The Importance of Cyber Hygiene for Families:

In today's world, where smartphones are pocket-sized computers and the internet is a gateway to information, entertainment, and social connection, our homes have transformed into digital playgrounds. As parents, you've witnessed firsthand how technology has revolutionized the way your children learn, communicate, and explore the world. While the digital landscape offers endless possibilities, it also presents new risks and challenges.

Cybersecurity breaches, online predators, cyberbullying, and identity theft are not just buzzwords; they are real threats that every family must confront. Just as you would teach your children to look both ways before crossing the street, it's crucial to impart the skills and knowledge necessary for safe and responsible online navigation.

Cyber hygiene is the foundation upon which digital safety is built. It encompasses a set of practices, habits, and strategies that can shield your family from the perils of the digital age. Think of it as the seatbelt in your car or the helmet on your child's head—a simple yet vital measure that can make all the difference in times of trouble.

The importance of cyber hygiene cannot be overstated. It's not merely about securing your devices and accounts; it's about safeguarding your peace of mind, your family's privacy, and your children's future. When you prioritize cyber hygiene, you empower yourself to embrace the digital age without fear and guide your children to become responsible digital citizens.

As we journey through the chapters of "Digital Guardians," you will discover practical insights, expert advice, and actionable strategies that will equip you to be the vigilant guardian your family needs in the digital world. We will explore how to secure your digital home, teach your children responsible online behavior, recognize and defend against cyber threats, and ensure that technology remains a force for good in your family's life.

So, let's embark on this transformative voyage together, where you'll emerge not just as parents but as Digital Guardians—protectors of your family's online well-being and champions of a safer, more connected future. Welcome to "Digital Guardians: A Guide to Cyber Hygiene for Parents."

A Note on Rapid Technological Changes:

Before we dive headfirst into the realm of cyber hygiene, it's important to acknowledge the ever-accelerating pace of technological evolution. Just as your children seem to grow inches overnight, so too does the digital world. New gadgets, applications, and online platforms appear almost daily, challenging us to keep up.

In the time it takes to finish this book, you can bet there will be new trends, devices, and potential risks on the digital horizon. This reality might seem daunting, but it's also an opportunity—a chance to embrace change and adapt, just as our ancestors learned to harness fire, build tools, and forge pathways in uncharted territories.

The rapidly changing landscape is precisely why understanding the fundamental principles of cyber hygiene is so crucial. These principles serve as your compass, guiding you through the uncharted waters of the digital age, regardless of the ever-shifting tides. They empower you not only to react to change but to anticipate and proactively protect your family in this dynamic environment.

This book aims to provide you with timeless insights and practical strategies while also acknowledging that adaptability is the key to successful digital guardianship. We'll explore how to foster an environment of continuous learning and adaptability within your family, ensuring that you remain well-equipped to tackle whatever the digital future may bring.

As we journey through these pages, remember that cyber hygiene is not just a destination but a lifelong journey. It's a journey that you, as a parent, have embarked upon to ensure a safer and more secure digital world for your family. So, let's embrace change and learning as we navigate this path together. Welcome to "Digital Guardians: A Guide to Cyber Hygiene for Parents."

Chapter 1: Understanding the Digital Landscape

The Internet's Impact on Parenting:

The advent of the internet has ushered in a transformative era, reshaping nearly every facet of our lives, including the way we parent. From the moment our children take their first steps into the digital world, we, as parents, are confronted with new challenges and opportunities that previous generations could scarcely have imagined.

As digital natives, our children often adapt to technology with an ease that leaves us both awed and, at times, apprehensive. We watch as they navigate smartphones, tablets, and laptops, seemingly fluent in the language of apps, social media, and online gaming from an early age. While their digital prowess is impressive, it also raises important questions about our role as parents in this evolving landscape.

The internet's impact on parenting is profound. It has changed the way we connect, communicate, and educate our children. It offers a wealth of information at our fingertips, enabling us to answer our children's curious questions with a few keystrokes. However, it also presents a vast digital playground, where our children interact with peers, explore the world, and discover their identities, often without the physical boundaries we had in our own childhoods.

As we navigate this digital landscape together, we'll explore the opportunities and challenges it presents. We'll delve into the ways the internet influences our children's development, their social interactions, and their education. We'll discuss the new roles we play as digital mentors, guides through the maze of online experiences, and protectors against the digital dangers that lurk in the shadows.

By understanding the internet's impact on parenting, we can better equip ourselves for the journey ahead. The digital world is a canvas upon which we can paint beautiful memories and experiences for our children, but it's also a place where we must remain vigilant, ensuring their safety and well-being.

In the chapters that follow, we'll delve deeper into the specifics of cyber hygiene and the tools and strategies that will empower you to become a confident and informed parent in the digital age. But first, let's continue our exploration of this digital landscape and how it has reshaped the parenting journey. Welcome to "Digital Guardians: A Guide to Cyber Hygiene for Parents."

The Digital Generation Gap:

In the timeless cycle of human existence, each generation passes its wisdom, values, and traditions to the next. But in today's world, there exists a profound digital generation gap—a gap that separates the experiences and perspectives of parents from those of their tech-savvy children.

The generation gap has always existed, marked by differences in music tastes, fashion choices, and even slang. However, the digital generation gap goes beyond superficial disparities; it's a divide defined by technology. As parents, many of us have vivid memories of growing up in a world where smartphones were nonexistent, the internet was in its infancy, and social media was yet to be conceived.

Our children, on the other hand, have never known a world without these digital marvels. To them, technology is as integral to life as the air they breathe. They communicate with emojis, express themselves through memes, and seek answers from a virtual assistant named Alexa. For them, screens are windows to a universe of information, entertainment, and social connections.

This generational contrast can sometimes lead to misunderstandings and challenges. Our children's ability to navigate the digital landscape can be baffling to us, while their reliance on screens may leave us concerned about their well-being. We find ourselves in a unique position—navigating a world where our children are the experts, and we are the learners.

Yet, the digital generation gap also presents an opportunity for growth and connection. As parents, we can bridge this divide by embracing technology alongside our children. We can learn from them as they learn from us. We can establish a dialogue where they teach us about the digital world, and we impart our wisdom about life's values and ethics.

In the chapters that follow, we'll explore strategies to close the digital generation gap, fostering understanding and cooperation between generations in this digital age. We'll discover how to harness the power of technology as a tool for learning, communication, and family bonding. Together, we'll navigate this unique terrain where the past and the future intersect.

As we delve deeper into the digital landscape and the challenges it poses, remember that being a digital guardian means understanding both the terrain and the travelers. So, let's continue our exploration of the digital world and the role of parents in guiding their children through it. Welcome to "Digital Guardians: A Guide to Cyber Hygiene for Parents."

Risks and Opportunities Online:
The digital landscape is a realm of contrasts, a place where remarkable opportunities coexist with significant risks. Just as the vast ocean can be a source of sustenance and adventure, it can also present perilous storms and uncharted depths. In the same way, the digital world holds both promise and uncertainty for families.

Opportunities:

In this ever-connected digital era, opportunities abound for families. The internet has shattered the boundaries of geography, offering a wealth of knowledge, culture, and experiences at our fingertips. It's a place where your child can explore history, access educational resources, and connect with peers worldwide. It's a canvas for creativity, where they can express themselves through art, music, and storytelling.

Online platforms facilitate communication and family bonding, allowing you to stay in touch with loved ones across the globe. You can share life's moments, from your child's first steps to their graduation, through photos and videos. The digital age has even brought forth new forms of family entertainment and learning, with interactive apps and games designed to educate and entertain.

Risks:

Yet, amid these remarkable opportunities, we must also acknowledge the digital risks that lurk in the shadows. The internet can be a breeding ground for cyberbullying, where hurtful words are typed in the absence of face-to-face accountability. It can expose our children to inappropriate content or individuals with malicious intentions. The digital world is not immune to scams, identity theft, and online predators, all of which pose real threats to families.

Moreover, the digital landscape can foster addictive behaviors, drawing children and adults alike into a never-ending cycle of screen time. The consequence can be a disconnect from the real world and the values that ground us.

As parents, our role is not to shield our children from the digital realm but to prepare them to navigate it safely. In the chapters ahead, we'll delve into the practices and principles of cyber hygiene—how to safeguard your family from digital risks while embracing the opportunities it offers.

We'll explore strategies for fostering a healthy relationship with technology, setting boundaries that respect screen time limits, and establishing open lines of communication with your children. By understanding the digital landscape, recognizing its potential, and mitigating its risks, you'll be well-equipped to guide your family through this dynamic journey.

So, let's continue our exploration of the digital landscape and discover how to harness its opportunities while guarding against its risks. Welcome to "Digital Guardians: A Guide to Cyber Hygiene for Parents."

Chapter 2: Building a Strong Foundation

The Role of Parents as Digital Role Models:

In the age of screens and keyboards, parents are not just caretakers but also digital role models. Children learn not only from what we say but from what we do. Our actions, habits, and attitudes toward technology set the stage for our children's own digital behaviors and beliefs.

Leading by Example:

Think of your digital presence as a mirror reflecting your values and behaviors to your children. When you model healthy digital habits, you lay the foundation for responsible online behavior in your family. Here are some ways parents can lead by example:

1. **Limit Screen Time**: Demonstrate moderation in your own screen time. Set boundaries for when and how you use digital devices and be mindful of your children's screen time as well.

2. **Prioritize Face-to-Face Interaction**: Encourage in-person conversations, family meals, and activities that don't involve screens. Show your children the importance of connecting with loved ones offline.

3. **Practice Digital Etiquette**: Use polite language and respectful behavior in your online interactions. Show your children how to communicate respectfully and empathetically, both online and offline.

4. **Share Positive Online Experiences**: Share your own positive online experiences, such as discovering new hobbies, learning from online courses, or connecting with friends and family. Encourage your children to explore the internet for similar opportunities.

5. **Protect Your Privacy**: Emphasize the importance of safeguarding personal information and respecting others' privacy online. Model strong password practices and teach your children to do the same.

6. **Critical Thinking**: Show your children how to critically evaluate online information and distinguish between credible sources and misinformation. Engage in fact-checking discussions together.

Open Communication:

Beyond modeling behavior, open communication is key to being effective digital role models. Create an environment where your children feel comfortable discussing their online experiences, concerns, and questions. Ask about their favorite apps, websites, and games, and show genuine interest in their digital world.

By fostering open dialogue, you empower your children to seek your guidance when they encounter challenges or uncertainties online. You become their trusted resource for navigating the digital landscape responsibly.

As we move forward in this journey through cyber hygiene for parents, remember that your role as a digital role model is not just about teaching rules but about instilling values. Your example will shape your children's digital identity and influence their behavior throughout their lives.

In the chapters that follow, we'll explore practical strategies and guidelines for establishing a strong digital foundation for your family. Together, we'll ensure that your role as a digital role model sets a positive standard for responsible online behavior.

So, let's continue building this strong foundation, where your actions speak volumes in the digital world you and your children share. Welcome to "Digital Guardians: A Guide to Cyber Hygiene for Parents."

Establishing Trust and Communication:

In the digital age, trust and communication are the cornerstones upon which a strong foundation for family cyber hygiene is built. As parents, your role extends beyond setting rules and monitoring screen time. It's about fostering an environment of trust and open communication that enables your children to navigate the digital world with confidence.

The Power of Trust:

Trust is the bedrock of a healthy parent-child relationship, and it's equally critical in the digital realm. When your children trust you, they are more likely to seek your guidance and confide in you when they encounter challenges online.

Establishing trust begins with consistency and reliability. Be consistent in your expectations and rules regarding digital behavior and be reliable in your support and availability when your children need assistance or advice.

Open Communication:

Open communication is the lifeline that connects parents and children in the digital age. It involves more than just talking—it's about listening, understanding, and responding with empathy. Here are some principles to guide open communication:

1. **Active Listening**: When your child talks about their digital experiences, give them your full attention. Listen without judgment and show that you value their perspective.

2. **Ask Open-Ended Questions**: Instead of asking yes/no questions, ask open-ended ones that encourage your children to express their thoughts and feelings. For example, "Tell me more about what happened online today."

3. **Empathize and Validate**: Validate your child's emotions and experiences. Let them know that you understand their feelings and concerns, even if you don't have all the answers.

4. **Share Your Own Experiences**: Be willing to share your own experiences, both positive and negative, from your time online. This can help your children relate to you and learn from your wisdom.

5. **Be Approachable**: Create an environment where your children feel comfortable coming to you with questions or concerns about their online experiences. Assure them that they won't face punishment for seeking guidance.

Digital Family Meetings:

Consider establishing regular "digital family meetings" where you discuss topics related to online safety, screen time, and responsible digital behavior. These meetings provide a dedicated space for open communication and ensure that everyone in the family is on the same page regarding digital rules and expectations.

By cultivating trust and open communication, you create a safe space for your children to share their digital experiences and seek guidance when needed. Your role as a parent extends beyond setting boundaries; it's about being a trusted advisor and confidant in the digital world.

In the chapters that follow, we'll explore specific strategies for setting digital boundaries and fostering responsible digital behavior. Together, we'll build a strong foundation that empowers your family to thrive in the digital age.

So, let's continue this journey of building trust and communication, where your connection with your children becomes a source of strength in the digital landscape. Welcome to "Digital Guardians: A Guide to Cyber Hygiene for Parents."

Setting Age-Appropriate Boundaries:

In the digital age, setting age-appropriate boundaries is essential to fostering a safe and healthy online environment for your children. Just as you baby-proofed your home when your child first started crawling, it's crucial to create a secure digital space as they embark on their online journey.

The Importance of Age-Appropriate Boundaries:

Age-appropriate boundaries serve several vital purposes:

1. **Safety**: Boundaries help protect your children from online risks such as cyberbullying, inappropriate content, and online predators.

2. **Healthy Development**: Setting limits on screen time and content ensures that your children have time for other activities, such as physical play, reading, and creative pursuits, which are crucial for their overall development.

3. **Balance**: Boundaries encourage a healthy balance between the digital world and the real world, preventing excessive screen time and its associated negative effects.

4. **Education**: By gradually introducing age-appropriate online activities, you can use technology as a tool for learning and skill development.

Establishing Age-Appropriate Boundaries:

1. **Know Your Child**: Recognize that every child is different. Understanding your child's maturity level, interests, and needs will help you determine appropriate boundaries.

2. **Start Early**: Introduce digital devices and online activities gradually, starting with age-appropriate content and supervised usage.

3. **Set Screen Time Limits**: Determine daily and weekly screen time limits that align with your family's values and your child's age. Consider using parental control tools to enforce these limits.

4. **Use Parental Controls**: Invest in parental control software or features provided by devices and apps to filter content, restrict access to certain websites, and monitor online activity.

5. **Educate Your Child**: Teach your child about responsible online behavior, privacy, and the potential risks they may encounter. Encourage them to ask for help if they encounter anything uncomfortable online.

6. **Lead by Example**: Show your children that you also respect screen time limits and use technology responsibly.

7. **Monitor and Adjust**: Regularly review and adjust boundaries as your child grows and gains more digital experience. What's appropriate for a 7-year-old may not be the same for a 14-year-old.

8. **Encourage Offline Activities**: Promote a variety of offline activities, such as sports, arts, and spending time with family and friends, to ensure a well-rounded childhood.

Balancing Independence and Protection:

Setting age-appropriate boundaries is a delicate balance between protecting your children and allowing them the independence to explore and learn. It's important to gradually increase freedom as your child demonstrates responsibility and a clear understanding of online risks.

In the chapters that follow, we'll delve deeper into strategies for age-appropriate boundaries and explore tools that can assist you in this critical aspect of parenting in the digital age. Together, we'll build a strong foundation that empowers your family to thrive in the digital landscape.

So, let's continue our journey of establishing age-appropriate boundaries, ensuring that your children's digital experiences are both safe and enriching. Welcome to "Digital Guardians: A Guide to Cyber Hygiene for Parents."

Chapter 3: Securing Your Digital Home

Protecting Your Home Network:

Your home network is the digital foundation upon which your family's online activities rest. Just as a sturdy house requires a strong foundation, your digital home needs a secure network to safeguard your online presence from potential threats. In this chapter, we'll explore the steps you can take to protect your home network.

Why Home Network Security Matters:

Imagine your home network as a virtual front door to your family's digital world. It's not just the gateway to the internet; it's the first line of defense against cyber threats. A secure home network ensures that your family's online interactions, personal information, and connected devices remain safe from prying eyes and malicious actors.

Securing Your Home Network:

1. **Router Security:**

    - Change Default Credentials: The first step in securing your home network is to change the default username and password of your router. These default credentials are often known to hackers and are a common point of entry for attacks.

    - Enable Encryption: Use WPA3 or WPA2 encryption to protect your Wi-Fi network. Encryption scrambles data transmitted over the network, making it unreadable to unauthorized users.

    - Update Firmware: Regularly update your router's firmware to patch known vulnerabilities and improve security.

2. **Network Name (SSID):**

    - Change the default network name (SSID) to something unique and unrelated to your personal information. Avoid using easily identifiable information like your name or address.

3. **Password Protection:**

    - Use a strong, unique password for your Wi-Fi network. Include a mix of uppercase and lowercase letters, numbers, and special characters. Avoid using easily guessable passwords like "password123."

4. **Guest Network:**

    - Set up a separate guest network for visitors to use. This network should have a different password from your main network and limited access to your devices and data.

5. **Firewall**:

   - Enable your router's firewall to filter incoming and outgoing traffic. A firewall adds an extra layer of protection by blocking potentially harmful data packets.

6. **Device Management**:

   - Keep a list of all devices connected to your network. Regularly review this list to ensure that only authorized devices are connected.

7. **Automatic Updates**:

   - Enable automatic updates for your router and connected devices. Manufacturers often release updates to patch security vulnerabilities.

8. **Network Segmentation**:

   - Consider segmenting your network into different zones for added security. For example, separate your smart home devices from your computers and personal data.

9. **VPN (Virtual Private Network)**:

   - Consider using a VPN for an added layer of security, especially when accessing the internet from public Wi-Fi networks.

10. **Monitoring Tools**:

    - Use network monitoring tools to keep an eye on the traffic on your network. Unusual activity can be a sign of a security breach.

By taking these steps to protect your home network, you'll create a safer digital environment for your family. In the chapters that follow, we'll explore additional strategies for safeguarding your family's online experiences and ensuring responsible digital behavior.

So, let's continue our journey of securing your digital home, starting with the foundation—the home network. Welcome to "Digital Guardians: A Guide to Cyber Hygiene for Parents."

Device Security for the Whole Family:

Your home is filled with digital devices, from smartphones and laptops to smart TVs and game consoles. Ensuring the security of these devices is crucial for safeguarding your family's digital life. In this chapter, we'll explore how to secure your devices effectively.

Device Security: A Collective Responsibility:

Device security is not solely the responsibility of one family member; it's a collective effort that involves everyone in the household. When each family member understands the importance of security and actively participates in maintaining it, your digital home becomes more resilient against cyber threats.

Securing Your Devices:

1. **Regular Updates**:

- Keep all devices, including operating systems, apps, and software, up to date with the latest security patches and updates. Enable automatic updates whenever possible.

2. **Strong, Unique Passwords**:

   - Encourage every family member to use strong, unique passwords for their devices and online accounts. Use a combination of letters, numbers, and special characters. Consider using a reputable password manager to help create and store complex passwords securely.

3. **Two-Factor Authentication (2FA)**:

   - Enable 2FA wherever possible, especially for accounts that contain sensitive information. 2FA adds an extra layer of security by requiring a secondary verification method, such as a text message or a biometric scan.

4. **Biometric Authentication**:

   - Whenever available, use biometric authentication methods like fingerprints or facial recognition to unlock devices. These methods are generally more secure than traditional passwords.

5. **Device Encryption**:

   - Enable encryption on devices like smartphones and laptops. This ensures that your data remains secure even if the device is lost or stolen.

6. **App Permissions**:

   - Regularly review and adjust app permissions on mobile devices. Only grant apps the permissions they need to function and be cautious about apps requesting access to unnecessary data.

7. **Screen Locks**:

   - Set up screen locks (PIN, password, or pattern) on all devices, especially smartphones and tablets. This provides an additional layer of protection against unauthorized access.

8. **Safe Browsing Habits**:

   - Teach your family safe browsing habits, including how to recognize phishing attempts, avoid suspicious websites, and verify the authenticity of online content.

9. **Device Tracking and Remote Wipe**:

   - Enable device tracking and remote wipe features for smartphones and tablets. These tools allow you to locate lost devices and erase their data remotely.

10. **Family Tech Talks**:

    - Regularly engage in discussions about device security with your family. Educate them about common threats and how to protect themselves.

11. **Parental Controls**:

    - Utilize parental control tools and software to manage and monitor your children's devices. These tools can help you set age-appropriate content restrictions and screen time limits.

12. **Secure Wi-Fi Network**:

    - Ensure that your home Wi-Fi network is secure (as discussed in the previous section). A secure network is the foundation of device security.

By implementing these device security practices and involving your entire family in maintaining a secure digital environment, you'll strengthen your defenses against cyber threats. In the chapters that follow, we'll explore additional strategies for promoting responsible digital behavior and protecting your family online.

So, let's continue our journey of securing your digital home by fortifying the devices that connect your family to the digital world. Welcome to "Digital Guardians: A Guide to Cyber Hygiene for Parents."

Safeguarding Personal Information:

In today's interconnected world, personal information is a valuable asset that needs vigilant protection. Your family's personal information is scattered across devices, accounts, and online platforms. Safeguarding this information is paramount to maintaining your digital home's security.

The Value of Personal Information:

Personal information includes everything from names, addresses, and phone numbers to social security numbers, financial records, and login credentials. Cybercriminals seek this data to commit identity theft, financial fraud, and other malicious activities. Protecting your personal information is essential to ensure your family's safety and privacy.

Safeguarding Personal Information:

1. **Secure Passwords**:

    - Encourage the use of strong, unique passwords for online accounts. Avoid easily guessable information like birthdays or names. A password manager can help generate and store complex passwords securely.

2. **Two-Factor Authentication (2FA)**:

    - Enable 2FA on accounts that offer this extra layer of security. This helps prevent unauthorized access even if someone obtains your password.

3. **Secure Storage**:

    - Safely store important documents and digital copies of sensitive information, such as passports or driver's licenses, in encrypted storage solutions or physical safes.

4. **Avoid Phishing Scams**:

- Educate your family about phishing scams, which often trick individuals into revealing personal information through fake emails or websites. Be cautious about clicking on links in unsolicited emails.

5. **Data Backups**:

   - Regularly back up important data and documents to secure, offline locations. In the event of data loss or ransomware attacks, having backups ensures you can recover your information.

6. **Privacy Settings**:

   - Review and adjust the privacy settings on social media and online accounts. Limit the amount of personal information shared publicly.

7. **Email and Messaging Security**:

   - Be cautious when sharing personal information via email or messaging apps. Verify the authenticity of recipients and use encrypted messaging services for sensitive conversations.

8. **Secure Wi-Fi Network**:

   - Ensure that your home Wi-Fi network is secure (as discussed earlier in this chapter). A secure network prevents unauthorized access to your personal data.

9. **Secure Device Disposal**:

   - When disposing of old devices, wipe their data thoroughly to prevent potential data breaches. Follow manufacturer guidelines for secure disposal.

10. **Online Shopping and Financial Transactions**:

    - Use secure, reputable websites for online shopping and financial transactions. Look for "https" in the website's URL, indicating a secure connection.

11. **Child Identity Protection**:

    - Monitor your children's online activities to ensure they do not inadvertently share personal information. Teach them about the importance of privacy and the risks of oversharing.

12. **Regular Audits**:

    - Periodically review your online accounts and devices to identify and address any security vulnerabilities.

Safeguarding personal information is an ongoing process that requires diligence and awareness. By following these practices and instilling them in your family's digital habits, you'll create a more secure and privacy-conscious environment for your loved ones.

In the chapters that follow, we'll explore additional strategies for responsible digital behavior and further fortifying your digital home. So, let's continue our journey of securing your digital home by protecting the invaluable asset of personal information. Welcome to "Digital Guardians: A Guide to Cyber Hygiene for Parents."

Chapter 4: Teaching Responsible Online Behavior

Navigating social media Safely:

Social media has become an integral part of our lives, providing a platform for connecting with friends, family, and the world. Teaching your family to navigate social media safely is an essential component of responsible online behavior.

Social Media's Role in Our Lives:

Social media platforms offer a space for self-expression, staying connected, and exploring new ideas. However, they also come with privacy risks, exposure to inappropriate content, and potential for cyberbullying. Balancing the benefits and challenges of social media is crucial for responsible use.

Guiding Your Family on social media:

1. **Age-Appropriate Access:**

   - Follow age restrictions set by social media platforms. Many platforms have age limits to ensure user safety and privacy.

2. **Privacy Settings:**

   - Review and adjust privacy settings on social media accounts. Encourage your family to limit the information shared publicly and to use strong, unique passwords.

3. **Think Before Sharing:**

   - Teach your family to think before sharing personal information or posting content online. Remind them that once something is posted, it can be challenging to remove it completely.

4. **Respectful Behavior:**

   - Emphasize the importance of respectful behavior online. Cyberbullying and hurtful comments can have serious consequences. Encourage your family to treat others online as they would in person.

5. **Report and Block:**

   - Teach your children how to report and block users who engage in harmful behavior. Most social media platforms provide tools for reporting and blocking abusive accounts.

6. **Digital Footprint Awareness:**

   - Help your family understand that their online actions leave a digital footprint. Colleges, employers, and others may view their online profiles, so it's essential to maintain a positive online image.

7. **Avoid Stranger Contacts:**

   - Advise your family not to accept friend requests or engage in conversations with strangers online. Explain the importance of verifying the identity of online contacts.

8. **Verification and Fact-Checking**:

    - Encourage critical thinking and fact-checking. Teach your family to verify the authenticity of information shared on social media before accepting it as truth.

9. **Balance Screen Time**:

    - Discuss the importance of balancing screen time between social media and other activities. Set screen time limits, especially for younger family members.

10. **Open Communication**:

    - Maintain open communication about your family's social media experiences. Encourage your children to come to you with any concerns or questions.

11. **Model Responsible Behavior**:

    - Set a positive example by using social media responsibly. Your children often learn by observing your online behavior.

12. **Cybersecurity Awareness**:

    - Educate your family about online scams and phishing attempts. Teach them to recognize suspicious messages or requests.

Navigating social media safely requires ongoing communication and education. By instilling these principles in your family's digital habits, you'll empower them to make responsible choices online and build a positive online presence.

In the chapters that follow, we'll continue to explore responsible digital behavior and how to navigate other aspects of the digital world securely. So, let's continue our journey of teaching responsible online behavior by focusing on the world of social media. Welcome to "Digital Guardians: A Guide to Cyber Hygiene for Parents."

Cyberbullying Awareness and Prevention:

Cyberbullying is a significant concern in today's digital age. It's crucial to equip your family with the knowledge and tools to recognize, prevent, and respond to cyberbullying effectively.

Understanding Cyberbullying:

Cyberbullying involves the use of digital communication tools to harass, threaten, or harm others intentionally. It can take various forms, including hurtful messages, online rumors, exclusion, and even blackmail. Cyberbullying can have severe emotional and psychological effects on victims.

Empowering Your Family Against Cyberbullying:

1. **Open Dialogue**:

    - Create an environment where your family feels comfortable discussing cyberbullying experiences or concerns. Encourage open dialogue about online interactions.

2. **Recognize Signs**:

- Teach your family to recognize signs of cyberbullying, such as sudden changes in mood, withdrawal from social activities, or reluctance to use digital devices.

3. **Document Evidence**:

   - In the event of cyberbullying, instruct your family to save evidence, including screenshots, messages, or any online content related to the incident. This evidence may be crucial for taking action.

4. **Block and Report**:

   - Emphasize the importance of blocking and reporting cyberbully on the respective platform. Many social media platforms and websites provide tools for doing so.

5. **Privacy Settings**:

   - Review and adjust privacy settings to limit the exposure to potential cyberbullies. Encourage your family to restrict access to personal information.

6. **Empathy and Kindness**:

   - Teach your family the value of empathy and kindness. Encourage them to stand up against cyberbullying by supporting victims and not engaging in harmful online behavior.

7. **Seek Support**:

   - If your family members experience cyberbullying, seek support from school counselors, teachers, or local authorities, depending on the severity of the situation.

8. **Online Reputation Management**:

   - Help your family understand that their online actions can impact their reputation. Encourage them to maintain a positive online presence and avoid engaging in cyberbullying themselves.

9. **Online Civility**:

   - Promote online civility and responsible digital behavior. Teach your family that online actions have real-world consequences.

10. **Resilience Building**:

    - Foster resilience in your family members by teaching them how to cope with cyberbullying and its emotional effects. Encourage them to reach out for emotional support.

11. **Report to the Platform**:

    - Encourage your family to report cyberbullying incidents to the respective platform or website administrators. These entities often take actions against cyberbullies.

12. **Legal Consequences**:

- Discuss the potential legal consequences of cyberbullying. Cyberbullying can be a crime in many jurisdictions, and individuals can face legal repercussions for their actions.

By raising awareness about cyberbullying and fostering a culture of empathy and responsible digital behavior, you'll help protect your family from the harmful effects of cyberbullying. Additionally, you'll contribute to creating a safer online environment for everyone.

In the chapters that follow, we'll continue to explore responsible online behavior and address various aspects of digital safety. So, let's continue our journey of teaching responsible online behavior by addressing the critical issue of cyberbullying. Welcome to "Digital Guardians: A Guide to Cyber Hygiene for Parents."

Recognizing Online Predators:

In the digital age, awareness of online predators is crucial for safeguarding your family's online experiences. Online predators are individuals who use the internet to exploit, groom, or harm children or vulnerable individuals. Educating your family about online predator risks is essential to responsible online behavior.

Understanding Online Predators:

Online predators can disguise themselves as peers, friends, or trustworthy individuals to manipulate their targets. They may attempt to establish trust and build relationships with the intention of exploiting or harming those they encounter online. Understanding their tactics is vital for recognizing potential threats.

Empowering Your Family Against Online Predators:

1. **Open Communication**:
    - Foster open communication within your family. Encourage your children to discuss their online interactions and friends with you.

2. **Recognize Warning Signs**:
    - Teach your family to recognize warning signs, such as:
        - Receiving unsolicited explicit messages or images.
        - Feeling pressured to share personal information.
        - Establishing secretive online relationships.
        - Noticing sudden changes in behavior, mood, or withdrawal from offline activities.

3. **Privacy Awareness**:
    - Educate your family about the importance of safeguarding personal information. Emphasize that sensitive details like addresses, phone numbers, and school information should never be shared online with strangers.

4. **Friendship Boundaries**:

- Encourage your family to limit online connections to people they know in real life. Explain that not everyone online is who they claim to be.

5. **Social Media Safety**:

   - Discuss the potential dangers of online friendships and emphasize the importance of privacy settings. Teach your family to avoid sharing personal details publicly on social media.

6. **Reporting Suspicious Activity**:

   - Teach your family to report any suspicious or uncomfortable online interactions to you or a trusted adult. You can then assess the situation and decide on appropriate actions.

7. **Online Gaming Safety**:

   - Monitor your children's online gaming activities and teach them about the risks associated with interacting with strangers during multiplayer games.

8. **Online Safety Education**:

   - Keep your family informed about the tactics online predators use. Explain that online relationships should never replace real-life friendships.

9. **Maintain Digital Boundaries**:

   - Encourage your family to set and maintain digital boundaries. They should feel comfortable ending online interactions that make them uncomfortable.

10. **Online Stranger Danger**:

    - Teach your children the concept of "stranger danger" online. Just as they would avoid speaking to strangers in person, they should exercise caution online.

11. **Trust Your Gut**:

    - Instill in your family the importance of trusting their instincts. If something feels off or uncomfortable online, they should take it seriously.

By raising awareness about online predators and empowering your family with the knowledge to recognize and respond to potential threats, you'll help create a safer online environment for your loved ones. Responsible online behavior includes being vigilant and cautious while fostering a sense of trust and communication within your family.

In the chapters that follow, we'll continue to explore responsible online behavior and address various aspects of digital safety. So, let's continue our journey of teaching responsible online behavior by addressing the risks of online predators. Welcome to "Digital Guardians: A Guide to Cyber Hygiene for Parents."

Chapter 5: Managing Screen Time and Digital Balance

Screen Time Guidelines:

As technology becomes more integrated into our daily lives, managing screen time and digital balance is essential for your family's well-being. In this chapter, we'll explore guidelines to help you strike the right balance between online and offline activities.

Setting Healthy Screen Time Limits:

1. **Age-Appropriate Guidelines**:

    - Consider age-appropriate screen time recommendations from reputable sources such as the American Academy of Pediatrics (AAP). These guidelines provide a starting point for balancing screen time with other activities.

2. **Customize to Your Family**:

    - Tailor screen time limits your family's needs and values. Every family is unique, so what works for one may not work for another. Consider factors like age, schoolwork, and recreational interests.

3. **Create a Family Media Plan**:

    - Develop a family media plan that outlines screen time rules and expectations. Include guidelines for weekdays, weekends, and holidays. Ensure that everyone in the family understands and agrees to these rules.

Balancing Screen Time:

4. **Prioritize Face-to-Face Interaction**:

    - Encourage regular face-to-face family interactions, such as meals, conversations, and activities, that do not involve screens. Create tech-free zones or times during the day for these activities.

5. **Limit Multitasking**:

    - Discourage excessive multitasking, which can lead to reduced attention and productivity. Encourage focused engagement with one screen or task at a time.

6. **Educational Screen Time**:

    - Acknowledge the value of educational screen time. Encourage your children to explore educational apps, online courses, and informative websites as part of their screen time.

7. **Physical Activity**:

    - Balance screen time with physical activity. Encourage outdoor play, sports, and exercise to promote a healthy lifestyle.

Quality over Quantity:

8. **Content Selection**:

- Monitor the quality of content your family consumes online. Encourage educational, age-appropriate, and value-driven content.

9. **Co-Viewing and Co-Playing**:

   - When possible, co-view or co-play with your children. This not only enhances their digital experiences but also provides an opportunity for bonding and discussion.

Leading by Example:

10. **Model Healthy Habits**:

    - Be a role model for your family. Demonstrate responsible screen time habits by managing your own digital usage and showing that you prioritize offline activities.

11. **Family Activities**:

    - Plan regular family activities that do not involve screens. These can include board games, nature outings, art projects, or cooking together.

Continuous Monitoring and Flexibility:

12. **Regular Reviews**:

    - Periodically review and adjust your family's screen time guidelines. As your children grow and their needs change, your screen time rules may need to adapt.

13. **Digital Detox**:

    - Consider occasional digital detoxes for the entire family. Choose a day or weekend to disconnect from screens and focus on alternative activities.

Balancing screen time is an ongoing process that requires flexibility and adaptability. The key is to find a healthy equilibrium that allows your family to benefit from technology while nurturing important offline connections and activities.

In the chapters that follow, we'll continue to explore strategies for responsible digital behavior and maintaining a balanced digital life. So, let's continue our journey by focusing on the critical aspect of managing screen time and digital balance. Welcome to "Digital Guardians: A Guide to Cyber Hygiene for Parents."

Encouraging Offline Activities:

While screen time has its place in the digital age, it's essential to promote a healthy balance by encouraging offline activities that foster creativity, physical well-being, and real-world connections. In this chapter, we'll explore strategies to inspire your family to engage in meaningful offline pursuits.

The Importance of Offline Activities:

Offline activities provide numerous benefits, including physical health, mental well-being, and the opportunity to nurture relationships. They help your family disconnect from screens and reconnect with the world around them.

Inspiring Offline Activities:

1. **Family Hobbies:**

   - Discover and engage in hobbies that the entire family can enjoy together. Whether it's gardening, hiking, cooking, or crafting, shared hobbies strengthen family bonds.

2. **Outdoor Exploration:**

   - Encourage outdoor adventures like hiking, biking, or camping. Nature offers a valuable opportunity to unplug and experience the beauty of the natural world.

3. **Reading:**

   - Foster a love for reading by providing access to a variety of books and creating a cozy reading nook in your home. Reading enhances literacy, vocabulary, and imagination.

4. **Arts and Creativity:**

   - Encourage artistic expression through activities like drawing, painting, music, or writing. Creative endeavors stimulate creativity and problem-solving skills.

5. **Physical Fitness:**

   - Prioritize physical fitness with family workouts, sports, or yoga sessions. Physical activity supports overall health and well-being.

6. **Community Involvement:**

   - Participate in community events, volunteering, or local clubs and organizations. Involvement in the community fosters a sense of belonging and civic responsibility.

7. **Cooking Together:**

   - Involve your family in meal preparation. Cooking together not only teaches valuable life skills but also provides an opportunity for quality family time.

8. **Board Games and Puzzles:**

   - Enjoy board games, puzzles, and brain-teasers as a family. These activities promote critical thinking and social interaction.

9. **Family Outings:**

   - Plan regular family outings to museums, zoos, theaters, and historical sites. These excursions offer both educational and recreational benefits.

10. **Screen-Free Days:**

    - Designate specific days or times for screen-free activities. Use this opportunity to explore new hobbies and spend quality time together.

Unplug and Connect:

11. **Digital-Free Bedrooms**:

    - Create tech-free zones in bedrooms to promote better sleep and reduce screen time before bedtime.

12. **Family Discussions**:

    - Initiate conversations with your family about the benefits of offline activities and the importance of balance.

Celebrating Achievements:

13. **Acknowledge Offline Achievements**:

    - Celebrate your family's offline accomplishments. Whether it's finishing a challenging puzzle or completing a hiking trail, recognition reinforces the value of offline activities.

Building a Balanced Life:

Balancing screen time with offline activities is an ongoing process. By actively promoting and participating in offline pursuits, you'll not only enhance your family's well-being but also cultivate a more balanced and fulfilling digital life.

In the chapters that follow, we'll continue to explore strategies for responsible digital behavior and maintaining a balanced digital life. So, let's continue our journey by emphasizing the importance of encouraging offline activities. Welcome to "Digital Guardians: A Guide to Cyber Hygiene for Parents."

Balancing Education and Entertainment:

In today's digital landscape, screens are not only a source of entertainment but also a powerful tool for education. Balancing these two aspects is essential for harnessing the educational benefits of technology while avoiding excessive screen time for entertainment.

The Dual Role of Screens:

1. **Education**:

    - Acknowledge the educational potential of screens. Digital devices can facilitate learning through access to online courses, educational apps, and informative websites.

2. **Entertainment**:

    - Understand the appeal of screens for entertainment, including video games, social media, and streaming services. Entertainment is a natural and enjoyable part of digital life.

Strategies for Balance:

1. **Scheduled Learning Time**:

    - Establish scheduled learning time when screens are used primarily for educational purposes. This can include online classes, research, and skill-building activities.

2. **Educational Apps and Games**:

- Incorporate educational apps and games into your family's screen time. Many interactive apps help children learn while having fun.

3. **Parental Guidance**:

   - Be actively involved in your children's online educational activities. Monitor their progress and ensure they are engaging with age-appropriate and reputable resources.

4. **Media Literacy**:

   - Teach your family media literacy skills, including critical thinking and fact-checking. These skills are crucial for discerning educational content and misinformation.

5. **Screen-Free Breaks**:

   - Introduce screen-free breaks throughout the day. Encourage physical activity, outdoor play, or other offline activities during these breaks.

6. **Media Balance**:

   - Strive for a healthy media balance by allocating specific time for educational and entertainment screen use. Discuss and agree upon screen time limits as a family.

7. **Quality Content Selection**:

   - Ensure that entertainment content aligns with your family's values. Choose age-appropriate and positive content that encourages learning or creativity.

8. **Family Discussions**:

   - Engage in conversations about the educational and entertainment aspects of screens. Encourage your family to share their interests and goals.

9. **Screen-Free Zones**:

   - Designate certain areas in your home as screen-free zones, such as the dining room or bedrooms. These spaces are reserved for family interactions and relaxation.

10. **Offline Activities**:

    - Promote a variety of offline activities, including hobbies, sports, and family outings. Offline experiences enrich your family's lives and complement screen time.

Balanced Screen Time Benefits:

Balancing education and entertainment on screens allow your family to enjoy the best of both worlds. Your children can learn valuable skills, explore their interests, and stay entertained while maintaining a healthy digital balance.

In the chapters that follow, we'll continue to explore strategies for responsible digital behavior and maintaining a balanced digital life. So, let's continue our journey by emphasizing the importance of balancing education and entertainment in the digital age. Welcome to "Digital Guardians: A Guide to Cyber Hygiene for Parents."

Chapter 6: Cyber Threats and How to Defend Against Them

Recognizing Phishing Attempts:

Phishing is a prevalent cyber threat that targets individuals through deceptive emails, messages, or websites with the aim of stealing sensitive information or infecting devices with malware. Teaching your family to recognize phishing attempts is crucial for their online safety.

Understanding Phishing:

1. **Email Phishing**: Phishing emails often mimic legitimate messages from trusted sources, such as banks, government agencies, or popular websites. They may contain links or attachments that lead to fake websites or malware downloads.

2. **Spear Phishing**: In spear phishing, attackers personalize their messages, often using information gathered from social media, to target specific individuals. These emails may appear more convincing because they seem tailored to the recipient.

3. **Smishing**: Smishing is a type of phishing that occurs through SMS or text messages. Scammers send fake messages with links to fraudulent websites or request sensitive information.

4. **Vishing**: Vishing involves phone calls where scammers impersonate legitimate organizations or government agencies to extract personal information or financial details from victims.

Empowering Your Family Against Phishing:

1. **Email Verification**:

    - Teach your family to verify the sender's email address. Genuine organizations use official domains; be cautious of misspelled or suspicious email addresses.

2. **Hover Over Links**:

    - Instruct your family to hover their mouse over links in emails to preview the destination URL. Be wary of shortened or suspicious links.

3. **Avoid Unsolicited Requests**:

    - Emphasize that legitimate organizations won't ask for sensitive information via email or text. Encourage your family to refrain from sharing personal details without verifying the request's authenticity.

4. **Check for Urgency and Threats**:

    - Phishing emails often create a sense of urgency or use threats to pressure recipients into taking action. Teach your family to be skeptical of such tactics.

5. **Be Cautious with Attachments**:

    - Advise against opening email attachments from unknown sources. Attachments can contain malware. Verify the sender's identity before opening any attachments.

6. **Verify Legitimate Contacts**:

- In cases of unsolicited requests, recommend that your family contact the organization directly through official channels to verify the request's legitimacy.

7. **Use Multi-Factor Authentication (MFA)**:

    - Enable MFA on accounts that offer it, especially for sensitive accounts like email and banking. MFA adds an extra layer of security.

8. **Keep Software Updated**:

    - Regularly update operating systems, browsers, and security software to protect against known vulnerabilities that phishers may exploit.

9. **Report Suspected Phishing**:

    - Encourage your family to report suspected phishing attempts to the organization being impersonated, as well as to the Anti-Phishing Working Group (APWG) or relevant authorities.

10. **Educate About Social Engineering**:

    - Explain the concept of social engineering and how attackers manipulate individuals into revealing information. Teach your family to be cautious when sharing information with strangers.

By educating your family about phishing techniques and providing them with tools to recognize and respond to phishing attempts, you'll help protect them from falling victim to these deceptive schemes. Phishing awareness is a crucial aspect of responsible digital behavior.

In the chapters that follow, we'll continue to explore strategies for defending against cyber threats and enhancing your family's cybersecurity knowledge. So, let's continue our journey by delving into the world of phishing and how to recognize these deceptive attempts. Welcome to "Digital Guardians: A Guide to Cyber Hygiene for Parents."

Malware and Ransomware Awareness:

Malware (malicious software) and ransomware are serious cyber threats that can compromise your family's digital security and privacy. Teaching your family to recognize and defend against these threats is essential for their online safety.

Understanding Malware and Ransomware:

1. **Malware**:

    - Malware is a broad term for software designed to harm, steal data, or gain unauthorized access to devices. It includes viruses, Trojans, worms, and spyware.

2. **Ransomware**:

    - Ransomware is a type of malware that encrypts files on a victim's device, rendering them inaccessible. Attackers demand a ransom payment in exchange for the decryption key.

Empowering Your Family Against Malware and Ransomware:

1. **Safe Downloads**:

    - Encourage your family to download software and apps only from reputable sources such as official app stores and legitimate websites. Avoid downloading software from unverified or suspicious sites.

2. **Anti-Malware Software**:

    - Install reputable anti-malware and antivirus software on all devices. Keep these security tools up to date to detect and remove malware threats.

3. **Software Updates**:

    - Stress the importance of keeping operating systems, software, and apps updated. Updates often include security patches that address known vulnerabilities.

4. **Email Caution**:

    - Instruct your family to be cautious when opening email attachments or clicking on links, even if the sender appears familiar. Malware often spreads through email.

5. **Avoiding Unknown Links**:

    - Teach your family not to click on unknown or suspicious links, especially in emails, social media messages, or text messages.

6. **Backup Data**:

    - Regularly back up important data and files to secure, offline storage. This ensures you can recover your data in case of a ransomware attack.

7. **Avoiding Suspicious Sites**:

    - Advise against visiting suspicious or illegal websites. These sites often distribute malware or ransomware.

8. **Phishing Awareness**:

    - Reinforce the importance of recognizing phishing attempts, as phishing emails often deliver malware.

9. **Avoid Pop-ups and Unwanted Downloads**:

    - Instruct your family to avoid clicking on pop-up ads or accepting unsolicited downloads. These can lead to malware installation.

10. **Secure Passwords**:

    - Emphasize the use of strong, unique passwords for all accounts, especially for sensitive ones like online banking. Weak passwords can be exploited by attackers.

11. **Ransomware Prevention**:

- Educate your family about ransomware and the dangers of paying ransoms. Paying does not guarantee the return of files, and it encourages criminal activity.

12. **Reporting Incidents**:

    - Encourage your family to report any suspicious activity, malware infections, or ransomware incidents to you or relevant authorities.

By raising awareness about malware and ransomware threats and providing your family with practical strategies for defense, you'll help protect their digital assets and personal information. Cybersecurity awareness is a fundamental component of responsible digital behavior.

In the chapters that follow, we'll continue to explore strategies for defending against cyber threats and enhancing your family's cybersecurity knowledge. So, let's continue our journey by delving into the world of malware and ransomware and how to defend against these malicious entities. Welcome to "Digital Guardians: A Guide to Cyber Hygiene for Parents."

Password Management and Two-Factor Authentication:

Effective password management and the use of two-factor authentication (2FA) are essential practices for safeguarding your family's online accounts and personal information in an increasingly digital world.

Password Management:

1. **Strong, Unique Passwords**:

    - Encourage your family to use strong, unique passwords for each online account. These passwords should be a mix of upper and lower-case letters, numbers, and symbols.

2. **Password Length**:

    - Stress the importance of longer passwords. Longer passwords are generally more secure. Aim for at least 12 characters.

3. **Avoid Common Words**:

    - Advise against using easily guessable passwords, such as "password123" or common phrases. Hackers often use dictionary attacks to crack these.

4. **Password Managers**:

    - Recommend using a reputable password manager. Password managers can generate and store complex passwords for each account, eliminating the need to remember them all.

5. **Frequent Password Changes**:

    - Encourage your family to change passwords regularly, especially for sensitive accounts like email and online banking.

6. **Security Questions**:

- Emphasize the importance of choosing security questions with answers that are not easily guessable or publicly available on social media.

Two-Factor Authentication (2FA):

1. **Enable 2FA:**

    - Instruct your family to enable 2FA on all accounts that offer this additional layer of security. 2FA typically involves receiving a one-time code via text message, app, or email when logging in.

2. **Authentication Apps:**

    - Recommend using authentication apps like Google Authenticator or Authy for 2FA instead of relying solely on text messages, which can be intercepted.

3. **Backup Codes:**

    - Explain the importance of saving backup codes provided during 2FA setup. These codes can help regain access to accounts if the primary 2FA method fails.

Password Hygiene:

1. **Avoid Password Sharing:**

    - Stress that passwords should never be shared, even among family members. Each person should have their own account credentials.

2. **Secure Storage:**

    - Teach your family to store passwords securely, whether in a password manager or a physical, locked location.

3. **Phishing Awareness:**

    - Continue educating your family about phishing attempts that may target their login credentials.

4. **Password Resets:**

    - Explain the process of password resets, emphasizing the need to verify the legitimacy of reset requests.

5. **Regular Audits:**

    - Periodically audit and update passwords for all accounts. Many password managers offer features to facilitate this process.

By adopting strong password practices and implementing 2FA wherever possible, your family will significantly enhance their online security. These practices are essential components of responsible digital behavior and can help protect against a variety of cyber threats.

In the chapters that follow, we'll continue to explore strategies for defending against cyber threats and enhancing your family's cybersecurity knowledge. So, let's continue our journey by focusing on the critical topics of password management and two-factor authentication. Welcome to "Digital Guardians: A Guide to Cyber Hygiene for Parents."

Chapter 7: Protecting Personal Data and Privacy

The Importance of Privacy Settings:

In an era of increasing digital connectivity, understanding and configuring privacy settings is crucial for safeguarding your family's personal data and online privacy. This chapter explores the significance of privacy settings and how to use them effectively.

Understanding Privacy Settings:

1. **Social Media Platforms:**

   - Explain that social media platforms offer various privacy settings that control who can see your family's posts, profile information, and contact details.

2. **Device Privacy:**

   - Devices, including smartphones and tablets, have privacy settings that determine app permissions, location sharing, and data access.

3. **Online Services:**

   - Many online services and websites allow users to adjust their privacy settings to control what data is collected and how it's used.

Empowering Your Family with Privacy Settings:

1. **Social Media Privacy:**

   - Encourage your family to review and adjust their social media privacy settings regularly. These settings can restrict access to personal information and posts.

2. **App Permissions:**

   - Explain the importance of reviewing app permissions on mobile devices. Only grant necessary permissions to apps, and revoke permissions that seem excessive.

3. **Location Services:**

   - Teach your family how to manage location services settings on their devices. Use these settings to limit which apps can access their location data.

4. **Browsing Privacy:**

   - Instruct your family on how to adjust browser privacy settings, including cookie management and ad tracking preferences.

5. **Search Engine Privacy:**

- Discuss the use of privacy-focused search engines that do not track user activity. Encourage your family to consider alternatives to mainstream search engines.

6. **Email Privacy**:

   - Emphasize the importance of email privacy settings, including enabling encryption and controlling spam filters.

7. **Cloud Storage**:

   - Explain the need to secure cloud storage accounts with strong passwords and two-factor authentication. Adjust sharing settings to restrict access to sensitive files.

8. **Online Accounts**:

   - Remind your family to regularly review the privacy settings of their online accounts, such as email, social media, and online shopping profiles.

Teaching Online Etiquette:

1. **Respect Others' Privacy**:

   - Stress the importance of respecting the privacy of others. Encourage your family not to share personal information about others without their consent.

2. **Think Before Posting**:

   - Teach your family to think critically before posting photos, videos, or personal details online. Once shared, this content can be challenging to retract.

Reinforce the Concept of Consent:

1. **Consent Matters**:

   - Explain that consent is a fundamental aspect of privacy. Teach your family to seek and give consent when sharing personal information or images.

Privacy and Digital Footprint:

1. **Digital Footprint Awareness**:

   - Educate your family about the concept of a digital footprint, emphasizing that online actions leave a trace. Encourage responsible online behavior to maintain a positive digital reputation.

By understanding the significance of privacy settings and how to configure them effectively, your family will have greater control over their online privacy and personal data. These practices are essential for maintaining a sense of security and control in the digital age.

In the chapters that follow, we'll continue to explore strategies for protecting personal data and privacy, further enhancing your family's cybersecurity knowledge. So, let's continue our journey by emphasizing the importance of privacy settings. Welcome to "Digital Guardians: A Guide to Cyber Hygiene for Parents."

Teaching Children About Online Privacy:

In an age where children grow up surrounded by digital devices and online interactions, it's crucial to educate them about online privacy. This chapter explores the importance of teaching children about safeguarding their personal data and privacy online.

The Significance of Online Privacy Education:

1. **Digital Literacy**: Explain that online privacy education is a fundamental aspect of digital literacy. It empowers children to navigate the digital world safely.

2. **Long-Term Impact**: Emphasize that online actions can have long-term consequences. What children share online today can affect their digital footprint and reputation in the future.

3. **Safety First**: Teach children that online privacy is essential for their safety. Personal information should be guarded just as they would protect themselves in the physical world.

Age-Appropriate Privacy Education:

1. **Start Early**: Begin teaching the basics of online privacy from a young age. Children can grasp concepts like not sharing personal information online or with strangers.

2. **Gradual Complexity**: As children grow, gradually introduce more complex privacy concepts, such as the importance of strong passwords and understanding privacy settings.

3. **Real-Life Analogies**: Use real-life analogies to explain online privacy. For instance, comparing sharing personal information online to sharing it with strangers on the street can help children understand.

Practical Privacy Lessons:

1. **Personal Information**: Teach children what constitutes personal information, including their full name, address, phone number, school, and more. Stress that this information should not be shared online without permission.

2. **Social Media Awareness**: Discuss the dangers of oversharing on social media. Encourage children to think before posting photos or personal details.

3. **Online Friends**: Explain the concept of online "friends" and why they should only connect with people they know in real life.

4. **Privacy Settings**: As children start using online platforms, show them how to configure privacy settings. Explain why these settings are important for controlling who can see their information.

5. **Password Education**: Teach children about strong, unique passwords. Show them how to create and manage passwords for online accounts.

6. **Recognizing Risks**: Discuss common online risks, such as cyberbullying and online predators. Teach children how to recognize and report such incidents.

7. **Seeking Help**: Encourage children to seek help from a trusted adult if they encounter anything online that makes them uncomfortable or if they have privacy-related questions.

Digital Empowerment:

1. **Positive Online Behavior**: Promote positive online behavior, empathy, and respect for others' privacy. Teach children that treating others online as they would in person is essential.

2. **Open Communication**: Maintain open communication with your children about their online experiences. Create an environment where they feel comfortable discussing any concerns or questions.

Leading by Example:

1. **Model Privacy Practices**: Be a role model for your children by practicing good online privacy habits yourself. Show them that privacy is a family value.

2. **Co-Explore**: Explore the digital world together. Use it as an opportunity to learn together, ask questions, and discover how to stay safe online.

By educating children about online privacy, you empower them to make informed decisions and protect themselves in the digital world. These lessons serve as a foundation for responsible digital behavior and maintaining their online safety.

In the chapters that follow, we'll continue to explore strategies for protecting personal data and privacy, further enhancing your family's cybersecurity knowledge. So, let's continue our journey by emphasizing the importance of teaching children about online privacy. Welcome to "Digital Guardians: A Guide to Cyber Hygiene for Parents."

Staying Informed About Data Privacy Laws:

In the ever-evolving digital landscape, it's essential to stay informed about data privacy laws and regulations that impact the way personal information is collected, used, and protected online. This chapter explores the significance of being aware of data privacy laws and how they affect your family's online activities.

The Importance of Data Privacy Laws:

1. **Legal Protections**: Explain that data privacy laws are in place to protect individuals' personal information from misuse, unauthorized access, and breaches.

2. **Accountability**: Data privacy laws hold organizations accountable for how they handle personal data. Understanding these laws empowers your family to demand transparency and compliance.

3. **Individual Rights**: Data privacy laws grant individuals rights over their data, such as the right to access their information, request its deletion, and opt out of data collection.

Why It Matters for Families:

1. **Children's Online Safety**: Data privacy laws often include provisions to protect children online, such as obtaining parental consent for data collection from minors.

2. **Online Shopping and Transactions**: Understanding data privacy laws is crucial for safe online shopping and financial transactions, as they dictate how your family's payment and personal information should be handled.

3. **Social Media and Apps**: Data privacy laws may impact the way social media platforms and apps collect and use personal data, affecting your family's online interactions.

Key Data Privacy Laws:

1. **General Data Protection Regulation (GDPR)**:

   - Explain that GDPR is a comprehensive data privacy law in the European Union (EU) that affects organizations worldwide if they handle EU citizens' data. It provides strict rules on consent, data breaches, and individual rights.

2. **Children's Online Privacy Protection Act (COPPA)**:

   - Discuss COPPA, a U.S. law aimed at protecting children's online privacy. It requires parental consent for the collection of data from children under 13.

3. **California Consumer Privacy Act (CCPA)**:

   - Describe CCPA, a California law that gives consumers more control over their personal data, including the right to request its deletion.

How to Stay Informed:

1. **Online Resources**:

   - Encourage your family to explore reputable online resources and government websites that provide information about data privacy laws and updates.

2. **News and Media**:

   - Stay updated through news articles, blogs, and reports that cover data privacy developments and legislative changes.

3. **Community Workshops**:

   - Attending community workshops or webinars on data privacy to learn from experts and ask questions.

Discussing Online Rights:

1. **Rights and Responsibilities**: Explain that understanding data privacy laws goes hand in hand with knowing your family's rights and responsibilities online.

2. **Consent and Opt-Outs**: Discuss how data privacy laws relate to obtaining consent for data collection and opting out of certain data practices.

Advocating for Privacy:

1. **Awareness and Advocacy**: Encourage your family to become advocates for digital privacy. Support efforts to strengthen data privacy regulations and hold organizations accountable for data breaches.

By staying informed about data privacy laws, your family can make informed decisions about how to navigate the digital world securely and responsibly. Knowledge of these laws empowers you to protect your personal data and advocate for your rights online.

In the chapters that follow, we'll continue to explore strategies for protecting personal data and privacy, further enhancing your family's cybersecurity knowledge. So, let's continue our journey by emphasizing the importance of staying informed about data privacy laws. Welcome to "Digital Guardians: A Guide to Cyber Hygiene for Parents."

Chapter 8: Apps, Games, and Online Content

Evaluating Apps and Games:

As digital consumers, your family encounters a vast array of apps, games, and online content. Teaching them how to evaluate these digital offerings is essential for ensuring a safe and enriching online experience.

Why Evaluating Apps and Games Matters:

1. **Quality and Safety**: Explain that evaluating apps and games helps determine their quality and safety. Not all digital content is suitable for all ages.

2. **Educational Value**: Emphasize the importance of choosing educational apps and games that support learning and skill development.

3. **Digital Citizenship**: Evaluating content fosters digital citizenship, teaching your family to be responsible and ethical users of digital resources.

How to Evaluate Apps and Games:

1. **Read Reviews**:

   - Encourage your family to read user reviews and expert opinions about the app or game. These reviews can provide insights into the user experience and potential issues.

2. **Check Ratings**:

   - Explain that app stores and game platforms often provide age ratings. Make sure your family understands these ratings and chooses content suitable for their age group.

3. **Trial Versions**:

   - Whenever possible, recommend trying out free or trial versions of apps and games before making a purchase. This allows your family to assess whether they enjoy the content.

4. **Educational Value**:

   - For educational apps and games, assess their alignment with educational goals and curricula. Look for content that reinforces skills or knowledge your family is interested in.

5. **Privacy Considerations**:

   - Discuss the app or game's privacy policy. Ensure it respects your family's data privacy and doesn't collect unnecessary information.

6. **In-App Purchases**:

- Caution your family about in-app purchases. Set clear guidelines on spending limits and ensure that children understand the concept of virtual purchases.

7. **Online Interactions**:

    - For apps and games with online features, discuss the potential for interactions with other users. Teach your family about safe online behavior, including not sharing personal information.

8. **Content Updates**:

    - Consider whether the app or game receives regular updates and support. Abandoned or outdated content may pose security risks.

9. **Community and Moderation**:

    - For online games and communities, investigate how well the platform moderates content and prevents inappropriate behavior.

Online Reviews and Resources:

1. **App Stores and Platforms**:

    - Encourage your family to explore app stores and gaming platforms for user reviews, ratings, and content descriptions.

2. **Educational Resources**:

    - Recommend educational websites and forums that provide insights into high-quality educational apps and games.

Setting Boundaries:

1. **Establish Time Limits**:

    - Set time limits for app and game usage, especially for younger family members. Balance screen time with other activities.

2. **Content Approval**:

    - For younger children, require approval from a parent or guardian before downloading or purchasing apps and games.

3. **Discuss Game Content**:

    - Engage your family in conversations about game content. Encourage them to share their experiences and concerns.

By teaching your family how to evaluate apps and games effectively, you empower them to make informed choices about the content they engage with online. This knowledge helps ensure a safe, enjoyable, and enriching digital experience for all family members.

n the chapters that follow, we'll continue to explore strategies for navigating the digital world and making responsible choices. So, let's continue our journey by emphasizing the importance of evaluating apps and games. Welcome to "Digital Guardians: A Guide to Cyber Hygiene for Parents."

Safe Streaming and Downloading:

Streaming and downloading content is a common part of the digital experience, but it comes with certain risks. Teaching your family how to stream and download content safely is crucial for their online safety and security.

Why Safe Streaming and Downloading Matters:

1. **Security**: Explain that safe streaming and downloading practices protect your family's devices from malware, viruses, and cyber threats.

2. **Privacy**: Emphasize the importance of safeguarding personal information while accessing online content, especially when signing up for streaming services.

3. **Content Legitimacy**: Teach your family to verify the legitimacy of streaming platforms and content sources to avoid illegal or pirated content.

How to Stream and Download Safely:

1. **Use Reputable Services**:

   - Recommend using well-known, reputable streaming platforms and online stores for downloading content. These services often have better security measures in place.

2. **Avoid Sketchy Websites**:

   - Caution your family against visiting sketchy or unknown websites that claim to offer free content. These sites may harbor malware or promote illegal downloads.

3. **Look for HTTPS**:

   - Teach your family to look for the "https://" prefix in website URLs, indicating a secure connection. Avoid websites without encryption.

4. **Beware of Pop-ups**:

   - Instruct your family to be cautious of pop-up ads and download buttons on websites. These can lead to unwanted downloads or malware.

5. **Read Permissions**:

   - When installing streaming or downloading apps, encourage your family to review the permissions the app requests. Be cautious of apps that request excessive access.

6. **Use Legal Sources**:

   - Emphasize that downloading copyrighted content without permission is illegal. Encourage your family to use legal sources and support content creators.

7. **Password Protection**:

- Stress the importance of using strong, unique passwords for streaming and download accounts to prevent unauthorized access.

8. **Verify Links**:

   - Teach your family to verify the legitimacy of links in emails or messages before clicking Phishing attempts can trick users into downloading malicious files.

9. **Ad Blockers**:

   - Consider using ad blockers to reduce exposure to potentially harmful online ads.

10. **Parental Controls**:

    - Implement parental controls on streaming platforms to restrict content access for children, ensuring age-appropriate content.

Regular Updates:

1. **Update Streaming Apps**:

   - Encourage your family to keep streaming and downloading apps updated to benefit from security patches and bug fixes.

2. **Keep Devices Updated**:

   - Regularly update operating systems and software on devices to maintain strong security.

Verify Content Legitimacy:

1. **Content Licensing**:

   - Explain how content licensing works and why it's essential to use licensed streaming platforms and avoid pirated content.

2. **Read User Reviews**:

   - Encourage your family to read user reviews and ratings for streaming platforms and content. This can help assess quality and legitimacy.

3. **Check for Copyright Notices**:

   - Teach your family to be aware of copyright notices and disclaimers on websites. These notices can indicate whether the content is legitimate.

By following these safe streaming and downloading practices, your family can enjoy digital content without compromising their security or privacy. These habits foster responsible online behavior and contribute to a safer digital environment.

In the chapters that follow, we'll continue to explore strategies for navigating the digital world and making responsible choices. So, let's continue our journey by emphasizing the importance of safe streaming and downloading. Welcome to "Digital Guardians: A Guide to Cyber Hygiene for Parents."

Online Learning and Educational Resources:
In today's digital age, online learning and educational resources play a significant role in expanding knowledge and skills. This chapter explores the benefits of online learning and how to make the most of educational resources while ensuring a safe and productive learning environment.

Why Online Learning and Educational Resources Matter:

1. **Access to Knowledge**: Explain that online learning opens doors to a vast array of knowledge, courses, and educational materials that may not be available locally.

2. **Skill Development**: Emphasize how online resources can help individuals acquire new skills, explore their interests, and stay informed.

3. **Flexible Learning**: Describe the flexibility of online learning, which allows your family to choose when and where to engage with educational content.

How to Use Online Learning Effectively:

1. **Choose Reputable Platforms**:

   - Recommend using well-established, reputable online learning platforms and educational websites. Research reviews and user experiences.

2. **Identify Learning Goals**:

   - Help your family set clear learning goals and objectives for online learning. Knowing what they want to achieve will guide their choices.

3. **Age-Appropriate Content**:

   - Ensure that the educational resources selected are age-appropriate for your family members. Some platforms offer content tailored to specific age groups.

4. **Interactivity**:

   - Look for interactive elements in educational resources, such as quizzes, simulations, or discussions, to enhance engagement and comprehension.

5. **Online Safety**:

   - Teach your family to practice online safety while using educational websites. Advise them not to share personal information or engage in risky online behavior.

6. **Schedule Learning Time**:

   - Create a schedule for online learning to ensure consistency. Allocate dedicated time for learning, just as you would for traditional schooling.

7. **Engage in Discussions**:

   - Encourage your family to engage in discussions or forums related to the educational content. This can foster deeper understanding and critical thinking.

8. **Supervision for Young Learners**:

    - For younger learners, provide supervision to ensure they navigate online learning safely and stay on track.

Diverse Learning Resources:

1. **Online Courses**:

    - Explore platforms that offer online courses on various subjects, from science and math to art and history.

2. **Educational Apps**:

    - Utilize educational apps designed to make learning enjoyable and interactive.

3. **Virtual Museums and Tours**:

    - Take virtual tours of museums, historical sites, and cultural landmarks worldwide.

4. **Educational YouTube Channels**:

    - Find educational YouTube channels that cover a wide range of topics, from science experiments to language learning.

5. **eBooks and Audiobooks**:

    - Access digital libraries and platforms offering eBooks and audiobooks for reading and listening enjoyment.

Assessment and Progress Tracking:

1. **Assessment Tools**:

    - Use assessment tools within educational resources to track progress and identify areas that may need additional attention.

2. **Feedback and Improvement**:

    - Encourage your family to welcome feedback and continuously strive for improvement in their online learning experiences.

Balancing Screen Time:

1. **Offline Activities**:

    - Promote a balance between online learning and offline activities, such as physical exercise, hobbies, and face-to-face interactions.

2. **Screen Time Guidelines**:

    - Follow recommended screen time guidelines, especially for children, to maintain a healthy balance between online and offline life.

Online learning and educational resources offer valuable opportunities for growth and development. By harnessing these resources effectively and responsibly, your family can enrich their knowledge and skills in an engaging and safe digital environment.

In the chapters that follow, we'll continue to explore strategies for navigating the digital world and making responsible choices. So, let's continue our journey by emphasizing the importance of online learning and educational resources. Welcome to "Digital Guardians: A Guide to Cyber Hygiene for Parents."

Chapter 9: Encouraging Digital Responsibility

Discussing Consequences and Accountability:

Fostering digital responsibility within your family involves frank discussions about the consequences of online actions and the importance of being accountable for their behavior in the digital realm.

Why Discussing Consequences and Accountability Matters:

1. **Awareness of Impact**: Explain that discussing consequences helps your family understand that their online actions can have real-world consequences for themselves and others.

2. **Ethical Behavior**: Emphasize the importance of ethical and responsible online behavior, which includes acknowledging the impact of one's actions.

3. **Safety and Security**: Teach your family that being accountable for their digital actions contributes to their online safety and security.

How to Discuss Consequences and Accountability:

1. **Open Dialogue:**

   - Maintain open and non-judgmental communication with your family members. Encourage them to share their online experiences, both positive and negative.

2. **Real-Life Examples:**

   - Share real-life examples of individuals facing consequences for inappropriate or harmful online actions. Discuss how such situations could have been avoided.

3. **Digital Footprint:**

   - Educate your family about the concept of a digital footprint. Explain that everything they do online leaves a trail that can impact their future.

4. **Privacy Violations:**

   - Discuss privacy violations and their consequences, such as the sharing of private photos or information without consent.

5. **Cyberbullying Awareness:**

   - Emphasize the harm caused by cyberbullying and the potential legal repercussions for those who engage in it.

6. **Laws and Regulations:**

   - Explain relevant laws and regulations, such as those related to online harassment, cyberbullying, and data privacy. Discuss the legal consequences of violating these laws.

7. **Preventing Harm**: Teach your family that taking responsibility for their online actions includes preventing harm to themselves and others.

Accountability in Online Interactions:

1. **Respectful Communication**:

    - Promote respectful communication and engagement in online interactions. Teach your family to think before they post or comment.

2. **Apologizing and Amending**:

    - Encourage your family to apologize and make amends if they realize they've hurt someone online. Acknowledging mistakes is a crucial step toward accountability.

3. **Report Inappropriate Behavior**:

    - Teach your family to report inappropriate or harmful online behavior when they encounter it, either to the platform administrators or to you as a parent.

Online Ethics and Values:

1. **Digital Citizenship**:

    - Emphasize that responsible digital citizenship involves upholding ethical values and treating others online with kindness and respect.

2. **Setting a Positive Example**:

    - Model responsible online behavior by demonstrating accountability and ethical conduct in your own digital interactions.

Empowering Responsibility:

1. **Encourage Empathy**:

    - Teach empathy and the ability to see situations from others' perspectives. This can help prevent hurtful online behavior.

2. **Critical Thinking**:

    - Promote critical thinking online by encouraging your family to question the accuracy and credibility of online information.

3. **Balanced Screen Time**:

    - Reinforce the importance of a balanced approach to screen time, ensuring that online activities do not negatively impact other responsibilities.

Positive Outcomes of Accountability:

1. **Trust and Respect**:

    - Explain that being accountable for one's actions builds trust and respect among family members and in the broader online community.

2. **Personal Growth**:

- Highlight that accountability fosters personal growth by encouraging self-reflection and learning from mistakes.

By discussing consequences and accountability openly and honestly, you empower your family to become responsible digital citizens who make informed, ethical, and considerate choices in the online world.

In the chapters that follow, we'll continue to explore strategies for encouraging digital responsibility and enhancing your family's cybersecurity knowledge. So, let's continue our journey by emphasizing the importance of discussing consequences and accountability. Welcome to "Digital Guardians: A Guide to Cyber Hygiene for Parents."

Encouraging Empathy and Kindness Online:

In today's interconnected world, fostering empathy and kindness in digital interactions is essential for creating a positive and respectful online community. This chapter explores the importance of these qualities and how to instill them in your family's online behavior.

Why Encouraging Empathy and Kindness Online Matters:

1. **Positive Online Culture**: Explain that empathy and kindness contribute to a more positive and welcoming online environment for everyone.

2. **Conflict Resolution**: Emphasize how these qualities help in resolving conflicts and misunderstandings peacefully, reducing online disputes.

3. **Mental Well-Being**: Discuss the impact of kindness and empathy on mental well-being, both for your family members and those they interact with online.

How to Encourage Empathy and Kindness Online:

1. **Lead by Example**:

   - Model empathetic and kind behavior in your own online interactions. Your family members often learn best by observing.

2. **Discuss Real-Life Scenarios**:

   - Share real-life examples of situations where kindness and empathy made a difference online. Likewise, discuss instances where a lack of these qualities led to problems.

3. **Online Bullying and Harassment**:

   - Address the issue of online bullying and harassment and how empathy can prevent and mitigate such behavior.

4. **Online Impact**:

   - Explain that words and actions online can have a lasting impact on others. Encourage your family to think before they post or comment.

5. **Teach Perspective-Taking**:

- Help your family practice perspective-taking, which involves seeing situations from others' viewpoints. This skill fosters empathy.

6. **Online Etiquette**:

   - Discuss the importance of online etiquette, including using respectful language, avoiding offensive content, and being considerate of diverse perspectives.

7. **Responding to Negative Behavior**:

   - Teach your family how to respond to negative behavior online with empathy and assertiveness rather than aggression.

Cyberbullying Awareness:

1. **Recognize Signs**:

   - Educate your family about the signs of cyberbullying and how to recognize when someone is being mistreated online.

2. **Reporting Mechanisms**:

   - Ensure your family knows how to report instances of cyberbullying to the appropriate authorities or platform administrators.

Positive Online Engagement:

1. **Engage in Constructive Conversations**:

   - Encourage your family to engage in meaningful and constructive online discussions. Discussing differing opinions respectfully can be a valuable learning experience.

2. **Promote Positivity**:

   - Share and promote positive content, stories, and initiatives that inspire kindness and empathy online.

Digital Empowerment:

1. **Digital Acts of Kindness**:

   - Encourage your family to perform digital acts of kindness, such as leaving positive comments, supporting online fundraisers, or sharing informative content.

2. **Support Mental Health**:

   - Highlight the importance of supporting mental health and well-being online. Teach your family to reach out to friends or family members who may be struggling.

Online Role Models:

1. **Identify Positive Role Models**:

- Help your family identify positive role models in the digital space who exemplify empathy, kindness, and responsible online behavior.

Encourage Offline Connections:

1. **Balance Screen Time**: Promote a balance between online and offline interactions. Encourage your family to spend quality time together and with friends in person.

2. **Kindness Beyond Screens**: Reinforce the idea that kindness and empathy should extend beyond digital interactions and into everyday life.

By emphasizing empathy and kindness in your family's online interactions, you contribute to a more compassionate and respectful online community. These qualities not only enhance your family's online experience but also contribute positively to the digital world as a whole.

In the chapters that follow, we'll continue to explore strategies for encouraging digital responsibility and enhancing your family's cybersecurity knowledge. So, let's continue our journey by emphasizing the importance of encouraging empathy and kindness online. Welcome to "Digital Guardians: A Guide to Cyber Hygiene for Parents."

Teaching Critical Thinking and Media Literacy:

In the era of digital information, teaching critical thinking and media literacy skills is essential for your family's ability to navigate the online world responsibly and discern fact from fiction.

Why Teaching Critical Thinking and Media Literacy Matters:

1. **Information Overload**: Explain that the internet is flooded with information, some of which may be misleading or false. Critical thinking helps your family sift through this sea of information.

2. **Fact-Checking**: Emphasize the importance of verifying the accuracy of information encountered online, especially before sharing it.

3. **Avoiding Misinformation**: Discuss the dangers of misinformation and how it can lead to poor decision-making and the spread of false beliefs.

How to Teach Critical Thinking and Media Literacy:

1. **Question Everything**:

   - Encourage your family to question the information they encounter online. Teach them that skepticism is healthy when assessing unfamiliar claims.

2. **Source Evaluation**:

   - Teach your family to evaluate the credibility of sources. Discuss indicators of trustworthy sources, such as expertise, reputation, and evidence.

3. **Fact-Checking Tools**:

   - Introduce fact-checking websites and tools that can help verify the accuracy of information.

4. **Media Bias Awareness**:

    - Discuss media bias and how it can influence the presentation of information. Encourage your family to consume news from diverse sources to gain a well-rounded perspective.

5. **Critical Reading and Watching**:

    - Teach your family to critically read articles, watch videos, and listen to podcasts by analyzing the content, authorship, and intent.

6. **Spotting Fake News**:

    - Educate your family on common signs of fake news, such as sensational headlines, poor grammar, or lack of credible sources.

7. **Emotions and Cognitive Biases**:

    - Discuss how emotions and cognitive biases can affect decision-making and critical thinking. Encourage your family to be aware of their own biases.

8. **Discussion and Debate**:

    - Engage your family in discussions and debates about current events and controversial topics. Encourage them to consider different viewpoints.

9. **Media Literacy Curriculum**:

    - Explore media literacy curricula and resources designed for different age groups and use them as part of your family's learning.

Online Safety and Privacy Considerations:

1. **Cybersecurity Awareness**:

    - Relate critical thinking to online safety by explaining how discerning malicious content or phishing attempts a cybersecurity skill is.

2. **Protecting Personal Information**:

    - Emphasize the importance of critical thinking when sharing personal information online. Teach your family to question why certain websites or apps request specific data.

Online Research Skills:

1. **Research Techniques**:

    - Teach your family effective online research techniques, including how to find reliable sources and cite them properly.

2. **Academic Integrity**:

    - Discuss the importance of academic integrity and avoiding plagiarism in online research and writing.

Positive Online Engagement:

1. **Respectful Discourse**: Encourage your family to engage in online discussions with respect for others' opinions and by presenting evidence to support their claims.

2. **Sharing Reliable Information**: Stress the importance of sharing reliable information and sources to contribute positively to online conversations.

Empowering Independence:

1. **Gradual Independence**:

   - Gradually empower your family members to apply critical thinking and media literacy skills independently as they grow and develop.

By teaching critical thinking and media literacy skills, you equip your family with the tools needed to navigate the digital world responsibly, make informed decisions, and contribute positively to online discourse.

In the chapters that follow, we'll continue to explore strategies for encouraging digital responsibility and enhancing your family's cybersecurity knowledge. So, let's continue our journey by emphasizing the importance of teaching critical thinking and media literacy. Welcome to "Digital Guardians: A Guide to Cyber Hygiene for Parents."

Chapter 10: Preparing for the Future

Keeping Up with Technological Changes:

In the fast-paced digital landscape, staying informed and adaptable is key to ensuring your family's long-term digital well-being. This chapter explores strategies for keeping up with technological changes and preparing for the future.

Why Keeping Up with Technological Changes Matters:

1. **Security and Safety**: Explain that technological changes often bring new cybersecurity threats. Staying updated helps your family protect their digital lives.

2. **Digital Competency**: Emphasize that adapting to new technologies fosters digital competency, which is essential for success in today's world.

3. **Education and Career**: Discuss how technological proficiency is increasingly important for education and future career opportunities.

How to Keep Up with Technological Changes:

1. **Continuous Learning**:

    - Instill a culture of continuous learning within your family. Emphasize that learning doesn't end with formal education.

2. **Online Courses and Workshops**:

    - Encourage your family to explore online courses, webinars, and workshops that cover emerging technologies and digital trends.

3. **Tech News and Blogs**:

    - Follow tech news websites and blogs that provide insights into the latest developments in the digital world.

4. **Podcasts and Videos**:

    - Explore podcasts and YouTube channels that explain complex technological concepts in an accessible manner.

5. **Online Forums and Communities**:

    - Join online forums and communities related to technology, where members share knowledge and discuss trends.

6. **Experimentation and Projects**:

    - Encourage your family to experiment with new technologies and embark on digital projects. Hands-on experience can be a powerful teacher.

7. **Coding and Programming**:

- Consider introducing coding and programming skills to your family, as these skills are increasingly valuable in many fields.

8. **Digital Literacy Curriculum**:

   - Look for comprehensive digital literacy curricula that cover a range of digital skills, from online safety to coding.

Adaptability and Resilience:

1. **Embrace Change**:

   - Foster an attitude of embracing change and adapting to new technologies rather than fearing them.

2. **Resilience in the Face of Challenges**:

   - Teach your family that setbacks and challenges are part of the learning process. Encourage resilience in the face of technological difficulties.

Tech-Savvy Parenting:

1. **Set a Tech-Savvy Example**:

   - Model tech-savvy behavior as a parent, demonstrating your own commitment to continuous learning and digital adaptability.

2. **Support Educational Endeavors**:

   - Support your children's educational pursuits related to technology, whether it's programming, robotics, or digital design.

Cybersecurity Awareness:

1. **Stay Informed about Cyber Threats**:

   - Keep up with cybersecurity news to understand emerging threats and vulnerabilities.

2. **Regularly Update Security Measures**:

   - Ensure that your family's devices and software are regularly updated with the latest security patches.

Balancing Technology Use:

1. **Set Screen Time Limits**:

   - Balance technology use with other activities, especially for children. Set reasonable screen time limits to maintain a healthy balance.

2. **Quality Over Quantity**:

   - Emphasize the importance of using technology mindfully and seeking quality digital experiences over excessive screen time.

The Future of Technology:

1. **Emerging Technologies:**

   - Discuss emerging technologies such as artificial intelligence (AI), virtual reality (VR), and blockchain. Consider how these technologies may impact your family's future.

2. **Ethical Considerations:**

   - Encourage discussions about the ethical implications of new technologies and how they should be used responsibly.

By instilling a proactive approach to keeping up with technological changes, your family can confidently navigate the evolving digital landscape, seize new opportunities, and address emerging challenges. This adaptability ensures that they are well-prepared for the future in an increasingly digital world.

As we conclude our journey through "Digital Guardians: A Guide to Cyber Hygiene for Parents," remember that digital responsibility and cybersecurity are ongoing commitments. Stay curious, stay informed, and continue nurturing a safe and responsible digital environment for your family.

Resources for Ongoing Learning:

To prepare for the ever-evolving digital landscape, having access to valuable resources for ongoing learning is essential. This chapter provides a list of resources that your family can tap into for continuous education and growth in the digital world.

1. Online Courses and Learning Platforms:

- **Coursera**: Offers a wide range of courses from top universities and institutions on various topics, including technology, cybersecurity, and digital skills.

- **edX**: Provides free online courses from universities and organizations worldwide, covering subjects like programming, data science, and cybersecurity.

- **Khan Academy**: Offers interactive lessons, practice exercises, and instructional videos on subjects ranging from mathematics to computer programming.

2. Tech News and Blogs:

- **TechCrunch**: A leading source for technology news and analysis, covering the latest trends, startups, and tech innovations.

- **Wired**: Features in-depth articles on technology, science, and culture, offering insights into emerging trends and their impact.

- **Ars Technica**: Focuses on in-depth technology news, analysis, and reviews, with a strong emphasis on cybersecurity.

3. Podcasts and YouTube Channels:

- **"Reply All" Podcast**: Explores internet culture, online communities, and digital mysteries.

- **TED Talks**: Features talks by experts on a wide range of topics, including technology, digital innovation, and cybersecurity.

- **Computerphile (YouTube)**: Offers informative videos on computer science, programming, and technology concepts.

4. Online Forums and Communities:

- **Reddit**: Contains numerous technology-related subreddits where you can discuss trends, ask questions, and share knowledge.

- **Stack Overflow**: A community of programmers and developers who help each other with coding and technical challenges.

5. Coding and Programming Resources:

- **Codecademy**: Offers interactive coding lessons and projects for beginners and advanced learners.

- **FreeCodeCamp**: Provides free coding challenges and projects to help learners build practical coding skills.

6. Cybersecurity Resources:

- **Cybrary**: Offers free and paid courses on cybersecurity, ethical hacking, and information security.

- **OWASP (Open Web Application Security Project)**: Provides resources, tools, and best practices for web application security.

7. Media Literacy and Critical Thinking:

- **MediaSmarts**: Offers resources and lesson plans for teaching media literacy and critical thinking skills.

- **NewsGuard**: A browser extension that rates the credibility of news websites, helping users identify reliable sources.

8. Digital Parenting and Family Resources:

- **Common Sense Media**: Provides reviews and resources for parents to make informed decisions about digital content for their children.

- **Family Online Safety Institute (FOSI)**: Offers guides, webinars, and research on online safety and digital parenting.

9. Online Educational Games and Apps:

- **PBS Kids**: Offers educational games and apps for children on various subjects, promoting learning through play.

- **Duolingo**: A language learning app suitable for all ages, helping users acquire new language skills.

10. Social Media Awareness:

- **Social Media Examiner**: Provides tips and resources for understanding and effectively using social media platforms.

- **ConnectSafely**: Offers guides and resources for promoting safe and responsible social media use.

11. Emerging Technology Exploration:

- **MIT Technology Review**: Covers the latest developments in emerging technologies, from AI and robotics to biotechnology.

- **Futurism**: Explores emerging technologies and their potential impact on society and the future.

12. Local Libraries and Educational Institutions:

- Don't forget to check with your local libraries and educational institutions for workshops, classes, and resources related to digital literacy and technology.

Encourage your family to explore these resources based on their interests and learning goals. By continuously expanding their digital knowledge and skills, they'll be better equipped to adapt to the ever-changing digital landscape and thrive in an increasingly tech-driven world.

As we conclude our journey through "Digital Guardians: A Guide to Cyber Hygiene for Parents," remember that learning is a lifelong endeavor, and the digital world offers endless opportunities for growth and discovery. Stay curious, stay safe, and continue empowering your family in the digital age.

Embracing Technology as a Tool:

In the final chapter of our journey, we'll explore the concept of embracing technology as a tool to enhance our lives and ensure a bright digital future for your family.

Why Embracing Technology as a Tool Matters:

1. **Empowerment**: Explain that technology, when used wisely, can empower your family members to achieve their goals and aspirations.

2. **Digital Confidence**: Emphasize that a positive attitude toward technology builds digital confidence, making your family better equipped to navigate the digital world.

3. **Problem-Solving**: Discuss how technology can be a valuable tool for problem-solving and creative expression in various aspects of life.

How to Embrace Technology as a Tool:

1. **Purposeful Technology Use:**

   - Encourage your family to use technology with purpose. Discuss how it can be a tool to enhance productivity, creativity, and communication.

2. **Life Enhancement:**

- Explore ways in which technology can enhance daily life, from simplifying tasks to expanding opportunities for learning and growth.

3. **Digital Well-Being**: Teach your family to strike a balance between technology use and offline experiences to maintain overall well-being.

4. **Innovation and Creativity**:

   - Inspire innovation and creativity by highlighting how technology can be a canvas for artistic expression, problem-solving, and invention.

5. **Learning and Skill Development**: Continue to promote continuous learning and skill development as key aspects of embracing technology as a tool.

Digital Tools for Education and Work:

1. **Online Learning**: Continue to encourage your family to explore online learning platforms to expand their knowledge and skills.

2. **Remote Work**: Discuss how technology enables remote work opportunities, promoting flexibility and career advancement.

Digital Tools for Creativity:

1. **Digital Art**: Explore digital art creation tools and platforms, allowing your family to express themselves artistically.

2. **Content Creation**: Encourage content creation through blogging, vlogging, or podcasting, fostering creativity and self-expression.

Digital Tools for Communication:

1. **Video Calls**: Highlight the importance of video calls and online communication tools for staying connected with loved ones, especially in today's globalized world.

2. **Collaboration**: Explore collaborative platforms that facilitate teamwork, project management, and idea sharing.

Digital Tools for Problem-Solving:

1. **Problem-Solving Apps**: Introduce problem-solving apps and software that help your family tackle challenges, from organizing tasks to tracking goals.

2. **Coding and Programming**: Continue to support coding and programming skills as tools for solving real-world problems and pursuing tech-related careers.

Digital Tools for Leisure and Entertainment:

1. **Entertainment Choices**: Discuss how technology offers a wide range of entertainment options, from streaming movies to playing video games, as forms of relaxation and enjoyment.

Balancing Technology Use:

1. **Mindful Consumption**: Emphasize the importance of mindful consumption, ensuring that technology serves as a tool rather than a distraction.

2. **Family Engagement**: Encourage family members to engage in offline activities together, fostering meaningful connections and shared experiences.

Digital Responsibility as Tool Users:

1. **Continued Digital Responsibility**: Reinforce the principles of digital responsibility and cyber hygiene as essential aspects of using technology as a tool.

2. **Respect and Kindness**: Discuss how technology can be a tool for promoting respect and kindness in digital interactions, creating a positive online community.

By embracing technology as a tool and maintaining a balanced and responsible approach to its use, your family can thrive in the digital age. Remember that technology is a tool at our disposal, and how we wield it can shape our present and future. May your family's digital journey be one of empowerment, innovation, and growth.

Thank you for joining us on this exploration of "Digital Guardians: A Guide to Cyber Hygiene for Parents." May your family's digital path be illuminated with knowledge, wisdom, and the confidence to navigate the ever-evolving digital landscape.

Conclusion:

Empowering Digital Guardians

As we conclude our journey through "Digital Guardians: A Guide to Cyber Hygiene for Parents," it's essential to reflect on the knowledge and insights gained, the strategies explored, and the commitment to becoming responsible and confident digital guardians.

In this book, we've ventured through the intricacies of the digital world, from understanding the digital landscape to securing our digital homes, teaching responsible online behavior, and preparing for the future. Along the way, we've embraced essential principles of cyber hygiene, such as cybersecurity awareness, privacy protection, and critical thinking.

The digital age is an ever-changing landscape, filled with opportunities and challenges. It offers boundless knowledge, connections, and conveniences, but it also presents risks that demand our vigilance and responsibility.

Empowering digital guardians is not merely about protecting against cyber threats; it's about nurturing a digital culture within our families that values responsibility, empathy, and continuous learning. It's about teaching our children and ourselves how to navigate the digital world confidently and ethically.

Here are the key takeaways from our journey:

1. Cyber Hygiene Matters:

- Cyber hygiene is the foundation of responsible digital citizenship. It includes practices that safeguard personal information, privacy, and digital well-being.

2. Digital Communication is Key:

- Effective communication within your family fosters trust and encourages open discussions about online experiences, challenges, and opportunities.

3. Education is Empowerment:

- Knowledge is your greatest defense in the digital world. Continuously educate yourself and your family about evolving digital threats and trends.

4. Responsible Digital Citizenship:

- Embrace the values of empathy, kindness, and accountability online. Encourage your family to be positive contributors to the digital community.

5. Adaptability is Vital:

- The digital landscape evolves rapidly. Embrace change, continuously update your skills, and stay informed about emerging technologies and trends.

6. Technology as a Tool:

- Technology is a tool to enhance our lives, solve problems, and create opportunities. Teach your family to harness technology wisely and responsibly.

7. Balance is Key:

- Maintain a balance between online and offline activities, ensuring that technology serves as a complement to, rather than a replacement for, other aspects of life.

8. Digital Responsibility is Ongoing:

- Digital responsibility is not a one-time endeavor. It's a lifelong commitment to protecting your family's digital well-being and fostering a positive digital culture.

As digital guardians, you have embarked on a journey that requires diligence, adaptability, and a commitment to nurturing a safe and responsible digital environment for your family. By embracing these principles and continuing to educate yourself and your loved ones, you empower your family to thrive in the digital age.

Thank you for joining us on this voyage and may your family's digital path be illuminated with knowledge, wisdom, and the confidence to navigate the ever-evolving digital landscape. You are the digital guardians of the future, and together, we can build a safer and more responsible digital world for generations to come.

Safe travels in the digital realm, and may your family be the stewards of a brighter digital future.

A Safe and Responsible Digital Future

As we bring our journey through "Digital Guardians: A Guide to Cyber Hygiene for Parents" to a close, it's time to reflect on the path we've walked and the vision we've crafted—a vision of a safe, responsible, and empowered digital future for your family.

In this book, we've delved into the intricate world of digital technology, from understanding the digital landscape to securing your digital home, teaching responsible online behavior, and preparing for the future. Along the way, we've discussed the fundamental principles of cyber hygiene, which serve as the pillars of responsible digital guardianship.

The digital age offers boundless opportunities for learning, connection, and innovation, but it also presents challenges that require vigilance, adaptability, and a strong commitment to digital responsibility.

Here are the key takeaways from our journey:

1. Cyber Hygiene:

- Cyber hygiene is the practice of maintaining digital health by safeguarding personal information, protecting privacy, and promoting responsible online behavior.

2. Family Communication:

- Open and honest communication within your family forms the bedrock of digital safety. Create an environment where your family can share their online experiences and challenges without fear of judgment.

3. Lifelong Learning:

- Knowledge is your most potent weapon in the digital world. Commit to continuous education and stay informed about evolving digital threats and trends.

4. Responsible Digital Citizenship:

- Instill values of empathy, kindness, and accountability in your family's digital interactions. Encourage them to be positive contributors to the online community.

5. Adaptability:

- The digital landscape evolves rapidly. Embrace change, continuously update your skills, and remain aware of emerging technologies and trends.

6. Technology as a Tool:

- Empower your family to harness technology as a tool for enhancing their lives, solving problems, and seizing opportunities responsibly.

7. Balance:

- Maintain a healthy balance between online and offline activities, ensuring that technology enhances, rather than hinders, other aspects of life.

8. Ongoing Responsibility:

- Digital responsibility is an ongoing commitment. Protect your family's digital well-being and cultivate a positive digital culture throughout their lives.

As digital guardians, you have embarked on a mission to create a safer, more responsible digital world for your family. By embracing these principles and continuing to educate yourselves and your loved ones, you are empowering your family to thrive in the digital age.

Thank you for joining us on this journey and may your family's digital path be illuminated with wisdom, knowledge, and the confidence to navigate the ever-evolving digital landscape. You are the architects of a brighter digital future, and together, we can build a world where technology enriches our lives while preserving our values and well-being.

Here's to a safe and responsible digital future for your family and all future generations.

Acknowledgments and Additional Resources

As we reach the conclusion of "Digital Guardians: A Guide to Cyber Hygiene for Parents," it's time to express our gratitude and provide you with additional resources to support your ongoing journey as digital guardians.

Acknowledgments:

First and foremost, we want to acknowledge the dedication and commitment you've shown in prioritizing your family's digital well-being. Your role as a digital guardian is crucial, and your proactive approach to learning and safeguarding your family in the digital age is commendable.

We also want to express our gratitude to the countless experts, educators, and organizations working tirelessly to promote digital literacy, online safety, and responsible digital citizenship. Your collective efforts contribute significantly to building a safer and more responsible digital world.

Additional Resources:

To further support your quest for digital knowledge and responsible online behavior, here are some additional resources you can explore:

1. Online Safety Resources:

- **National Cyber Security Centre (NCSC)**: Offers a range of resources, including guidance on cybersecurity and online safety for families.
- **Stay Safe Online**: Provides tips, resources, and guides to enhance online safety for individuals and families.

2. Parental Control and Monitoring Tools:

- **Norton Family**: A parental control and monitoring software that helps you supervise your child's online activities.
- **Qustodio**: Offers a suite of parental control features to manage screen time, filter content, and monitor social media.

3. Online Safety Education for Kids:

- **NetSmartz Kids**: Provides age-appropriate resources and games to educate children about online safety.
- **CyberSense and Nonsense**: An interactive online game that teaches kids about online safety.

4. Books on Digital Parenting:

- **"The Cyber Effect" by Mary Aiken**: Explores the impact of technology on children's development and provides insights for parents.
- **"Screenwise" by Devorah Heitner**: Offers guidance on raising kids in the digital age with a focus on responsible technology use.

5. Online Courses and Workshops:

- **Coursera**: Features courses on digital parenting, cybersecurity, and digital literacy.
- **edX**: Provides access to online courses on internet safety, digital skills, and more.

6. Local Community Resources:

Don't forget to explore local resources, such as parenting groups, school workshops, and libraries, which may offer support and educational opportunities related to digital parenting and online safety.

7. Stay Informed:

Keep up to date with the latest developments in the digital world by following technology news websites, blogs, and podcasts. Stay curious and explore emerging technologies to remain digitally literate.

Closing Thoughts:

In closing, we commend you for your commitment to becoming a digital guardian for your family. Your dedication to their digital well-being is a valuable gift, and by nurturing a responsible and safe digital environment, you are shaping a brighter future for them in the digital age.

Remember that your journey as a digital guardian is ongoing, and learning and adapting are key. Stay curious, stay vigilant, and stay connected with your family as you navigate the ever-changing digital landscape together.

Thank you for joining us on this voyage through "Digital Guardians." May your family's digital path be filled with knowledge, wisdom, and a commitment to responsible and empowered digital citizenship.

Best wishes for a safe and fulfilling digital future for you and your loved ones.

About the Author:

L. Randolf Bryant is a veteran currently working in the government sector curious about threats and problem-solving that seems to change and evolve as much as the wind blows.